FIRST AMONG EQUALS

Scharada Dubey is a writer, internet consultant and Tarot practitioner. She has won several writing awards and her books for children include the travelogues *Footloose on the West Coast, Malwa on My Mind* and *A Necessary Journey.*

FIRST AMONG EQUALS
Presidents of India 1950 to 2009

Scharada Dubey

_w_
Westland Ltd

westland ltd.
61, Silverline Building, Alapakkam Main Road, Maduravoyal,
Chennai 600 095
93, 1st Floor, Sham Lal Road, Daryaganj, New Delhi 110 002

Frist published by westland ltd 2009

10 9 8 7 6 5 4 3 2 1

ISBN: 978-81-89975-53-1

Illustrations: Rahul Krishnan

Typeset in RotisSemiSans by Mindways Design, New Delhi

Contents

Introduction

The head of the Indian State, the president of India, is a significant constitutional post. Occupants of this post, however, remain largely outside the public gaze, with their role assuming great importance during periods of crises and national debate. Unfortunately, the knowledge that most students and Indians have about their presidents remains sketchy at best. This is largely because, unlike the prime minister, the president is not elected by direct popular mandate. Instead, our head of State is brought into power through electoral colleges consisting of legislators from the Centre and states.

Many personalities from different regions, classes, vocations and backgrounds have made their way into Rashtrapati Bhavan. What set these personalities apart from their peers? What special qualities did they bring to their office?

What crises did the country face during their terms and how were these resolved? These are some of the questions whose answers can be found in the profiles of our presidents. While all the men and women who have held office as president have been described, profiles of M. Hidayatullah who served as the chief justice of India and was acting president on two occasions, and B.D. Jatti, who was acting president in 1977, have not been included.

One of the factors that prevents us from making a more meaningful contribution to the society in which we live is an incomplete understanding of our history, politics and the social conditions that shape it. Learning about the lives of our presidents does something to address this gap. I am grateful to Westland Ltd for giving me this canvas to work on, and to Deepthi Talwar, my editor, for her patient encouragement during the entire project. I hope the book it has resulted in will bring inspiration and insight to young and older readers.

Scharada Dubey

Rajendra Prasad (1884–1963)

First Choice for President
Rajendra Prasad

Term of Office: 26 January 1950–13 May 1962

If there was one leader who embodied Gandhian principles and values as completely as Mahatma Gandhi himself, it was Rajendra Prasad. When the Congress was going through an internal evaluation in 1922, about whether it was right to act in accordance with Gandhian methods and principles, the stalwarts of the party were persuaded to stay with Gandhism due to the personality of Gandhiji's most devoted contemporary.

About Prasad, Gandhiji once said, 'There is at least one man who would not hesitate to take the cup of poison from my hands.' This freedom-fighter was such an upright and honest figure in the Congress, that Motilal Nehru remarked about him in January 1923, 'We have given a fair trial to Gandhism for over two years. It seems to me that the only good result it has yielded — I do not say it will not yield better or more results — is Babu Rajendra Prasad.'

Rajendra Prasad, the first president of independent India, was born on 3 December 1884 in Zeradei, in the Siwan district of Bihar near Chapra. Prasad's great uncle, Chaudhur Lal, was the dewan of the Hathwa Raj, a highly respected, honest and efficient gentleman who built up the land holdings of Prasad's family and was a well-known zamindar. His nephew, Mahadev Sahay, was Prasad's father, a man who lived in rustic surroundings and yet was a scholar of Persian and Sanskrit. He had also cultivated several hobbies like wrestling and horticulture which he pursued with passion, and his considerable knowledge of Ayurvedic and Unani medicine made the people of the area flock to him for treatment. His wife, Kamleshwari Devi, was a devout lady who daily told stories from the *Ramayana* to her young son Rajendra. These tales, so much a part of his childhood, stayed with Rajendra Babu well into his adult life, when the *Ramcharitmanas* by Tulsidas became his constant companion.

Inspired more by high ideals than the lure of wealth or power, Prasad's family lived simply. They mixed freely with all their fellow villagers, without allowing disparities to come in the way of social interactions. Prasad's early life in the village was an enjoyable experience of peace and quiet, festivals and fairs. It was this experience of rural India that would stay with him as an ideal vision of the village and life in the rural milieu.

When he was five years old, Prasad was placed under the instruction of a maulavi who taught him Persian. He also learnt Hindi and arithmetic and later went on to study at the Chapra Zilla School. A few years later he left Chapra to study at R.K. Ghosh's Academy in Patna, where he lived with his elder brother, Mahendra Prasad, who was then studying at Patna College. However, Rajendra Prasad completed his school education from the Chapra Zilla School because his brother moved to Calcutta in 1897. At the age of eighteen he passed the Entrance examination of Calcutta University in 1902, standing first among all entrants. This was a truly remarkable scholastic achievement, because the entrance examination encompassed students from places as far apart as Sadiya, the easternmost frontier of British India, to a little beyond Peshawar on the northwestern side.

Prasad was married at the age of thirteen to Rajbanshi Devi. When he had obtained admission to Calcutta University, he moved to Calcutta and began sharing a room with his elder brother at Eden Hindu Hostel, attending classes at Presidency College. He became very popular and well-known in a remarkably short time, even though there were not many students from Bihar at the time in Calcutta. In 1904 he contested and won the first annual election for the post of secretary of the college union against a senior student belonging to a rich and influential family. He was then a third-year student. The election result — victory by more than a thousand votes against a mere seven for the other candidate — so astonished Dr P.K. Roy, the principal of the college, that he was forced to enquire as to what it was that made Prasad so popular.

Choosing to study Arts, Prasad had a remarkably distinguished academic career, with a First Class in MA and another First in LLM. However, with the idea of swadeshi occupying his mind and heart, he was not interested in becoming a professor. His brother had introduced him to the ideas of the freedom struggle, and he joined the Dawn Society while in college. This society, run by Satish Chandra Mukherjee, Sister Nivedita, Surendranath Banerjee and many other luminaries, conducted debating and essay-writing competitions on many current topics, and young Prasad won many of the prizes. Stirred by the processions, slogans and speeches of the time, he collected the Bihari students in Calcutta and formed the Bihari Students' Conference in 1908. This was the organisation that produced and nurtured almost the entire political leadership of Bihar in the 1920s.

In 1910, Prasad met Gopal Krishna Gokhale, a towering leader of the time. Gokhale would later invite him to join the Servants of India Society in Pune. Prasad set himself up as a legal practitioner in Calcutta in 1911, and also joined the Indian National Congress, where he was elected to the All India Congress Committee. When he received Gopal Krishna Gokhale's invitation to go to Pune, he was very much tempted to take up the offer. Prasad's family estate was in bad shape at this time, and his family looked upon him to restore the family fortunes. Unable to have a direct conversation with his elder brother, Prasad sought his permission to go to Pune through a letter, in which he wrote: 'Ambitions I have none except to be of some service to the Motherland'. His brother reacted with so much anguish to his request that Prasad decided to stay back to take care of his family affairs.

Things took a more difficult turn at the time because his mother died and his only sister, Bhagwati Devi, fifteen years older than him, returned to her parents' home as a widow. From then on, it was this sister who took the place of Prasad's mother in his life. She nurtured him in the years leading up to his establishment as a young lawyer in the Patna high court.

Prasad's legal career was exceptional not only because of his incisive intellect and phenomenal memory, but the complete integrity and honesty that marked all his actions. It was this purity of character that drew respect for him from his colleagues, clients and judges. His knowledge of the law was so all-encompassing that when his opponents in court faltered while trying to cite a precedent to prove their argument, the judges turned to Prasad to do it for them!

Soon after he became a lawyer, Prasad met Mahatma Gandhi and was drawn into the Indian freedom struggle. He collected volunteers and went to Champaran, where he was completely overcome by Mahatma Gandhi's courage and unshakable commitment to the truth. Following this, Prasad threw himself into the movement for India's independence with enthusiasm, resigning as a senator of Calcutta University in 1921, in order to devote more time for such activities. When Mahatma Gandhi called upon Indians to boycott Western education, Prasad asked his son Mrityunjaya, a brilliant student, to drop out of the university and begin studying at Bihar Vidyapeeth, an institution he and his colleagues had set up along the lines of a traditional Indian institution.

Prasad's efforts during the freedom struggle brought out his role as an excellent communicator. He wrote articles and collected funds for the journals *Searchlight* and *Desh*. He toured vast areas, meeting people, giving many lectures and urging those whom he met to join the freedom struggle.

Prasad was also very active in relief work. When floods devastated large areas of Bihar and Bengal in 1914, Prasad and his colleagues worked actively to help the affected people. Years later

Prasad would be in jail when the earthquake of Bihar occurred on 15 January 1934. As soon as he was released, he set himself the task of raising funds for the earthquake-affected. It is to his great credit that the amount of money he raised, over Rs 38 lakhs, was three times the Viceroy's fund for the same purpose. In 1935, during the Quetta earthquake, Prasad set up relief committees in the Sindh and Punjab areas of what is now Pakistan. During all these years, Prasad suffered several terms of rigorous imprisonment under the British, which took a toll on his health. He was troubled by chronic asthma. Besides, he faced many difficulties for want of a regular income of his own. In spite of these difficulties he did not accept any financial assistance from the Congress or from any other source and depended mostly on his elder brother.

The remaining years of Prasad's life were to see him emerge as a key and well-respected member of the Congress. He was elected president of the Indian National Congress during the Bombay session in October 1934. He again became president when Netaji Subhash Chandra Bose resigned in 1939.

In 1937, when the Congress ministries were formed in different regions of India, Prasad, along with Sardar Vallabhbhai Patel and Maulana Abul Kalam Azad, was part of the parliamentary board which provided the guidance for ministry-formation. Prasad was also the president of the Constituent Assembly of India, the leaders of which laid the foundation for India's Constitution. With stalwarts like Baba Ambedkar and Maulana Azad among others, this Assembly was guided with exemplary patience and skill by Rajendra Babu. He conducted matters so that there could be consensus and all members took part in full, free and frank discussions. At the end of the Assembly's sessions, his colleagues showered rich tributes on him.

As Food and Agriculture minister, Prasad attempted to repair the web of village life disrupted by industrial progress. He wanted Gandhian values to be at the core of village life, with self-discipline, village industries and a sense of community. He coined the slogan 'Grow More Food' for the Food ministry, and a nation-wide campaign was initiated under his guidance.

Prasad became the first president of the Republic of India in 1950, an elevation that some considered inevitable. There were some, however, who thought him unfit for the ceremonial office because he lived and dressed like a peasant, and was unconcerned about what people said of him. Regardless of the differing points of view about his taking up residence at Rashtrapati Bhavan, to all those who had intimately followed the history of the Indian struggle for independence, there was only one choice for president, and that was Rajendra Prasad.

Fulfilling his role as president, Prasad moulded policies and actions in such a moderate and unobtrusive manner that his occasional differences with Prime Minister Nehru never became the subject of controversy or speculation.

In later years he was doubly bereaved – on the night of 25 January 1960, on the eve of Republic Day, he lost his elder sister Bhagwati Devi, and later, in September 1962, his wife Rajbanshi Devi died. These losses, and the events leading to the India–China war of 1962, left him shaken and affected his health. That year, after twelve years as president, he announced his decision to retire. He was subsequently awarded the Bharat Ratna, the nation's highest civilian award. On 28 February 1963, he passed away.

Rajendra Babu, beloved of vast numbers of his countrymen, was called 'Desh Ratna' by them as a mark of affection. His purity of character made Jawaharlal Nehru call him the symbol of Bharat and describe how he found 'truth looking at you through those (Rajendra Babu's) eyes'.

Sarvapalli Radhakrishnan (1888–1975)

Philosopher in Office
Sarvapalli Radhakrishnan

Term of Office: 13 May 1962–13 May 1967

When we meet people from other countries and cultures, what sometimes strikes us is how different their view of the world, and of life, is from our own. Even though today's world is dominated more by a single, consumer-driven culture, there are still fundamental differences between how an Indian may think, and how a South African or Australian may think.

Dr Sarvapalli Radhakrishnan, the second president of independent India, was a great thinker, scholar and writer who studied the deep origins of Indian and Western philosophy and successfully created a bridge between the two. It is difficult to describe the lifetime achievements of Dr Radhakrishnan without falling into the danger of exaggeration. His life was a long journey of lively scholarship and philosophy that found an echo in the lives of ordinary people, and he was honoured and respected by some of the best-known institutions in the world. Yet, he retained the simplicity and austerity that mark the truly great.

Dr Radhakrishnan was born on 5 September 1888 into a Telugu Brahmin family, in Tiruttani, a well-known pilgrim town in Tamil Nadu famous for its Murugan temple. He was the second son of Veera Samayya, a tehsildar in a zamindari. His father's administrative post made the family relatively prosperous in the rural social and economic structure of that time. The atmosphere at Radhakrishnan's home was very loving and encouraging for him as he was growing up. Like any typical middle-class, respectable Hindu Brahmin family, his parents had a high regard for education, and were determined that their son receive the best schooling. They were also well-steeped in the religion and values of devout Hindus, imparting a gentle, tolerant and disciplined approach to life to him. These seeds would bear precious fruit in Radhakrishnan's adult life.

The first eight years of Radhakrishnan's life in the town of temples and pilgrims were very happy and carefree. The peace and calm of the countryside, as well as the love and affection from his parents and extended family, was what would form his enduring memories of these days and mould his character for good. Radhakrishnan clearly enjoyed every form of learning and showed a bright and enquiring disposition, thirsty for knowledge. What was most significant was that his parents, although orthodox, chose to send him to Christian missionary schools and colleges, which at that time imparted the best education. He studied at the Lutheran Mission School, Tirupati, from 1896 to 1900, at Vellore College, Vellore, from 1900 to 1904 and at Madras Christian College from 1904 to 1908.

His marriage was arranged, in the manner of those times, when he was a mere eighteen year old. Thus, he married Sivakamamma in 1906 when he was still a student. This would be an enduring and happy union for fifty years till Sivakamamma's death in 1956.

The couple was blessed with five daughters and a son.

Being educated in Christian missionary institutions exposed young Radhakrishnan to the discipline, punctuality, order and scientific temperament of the West, even as it reinforced the values he had imbibed from his childhood environment. He was fortunate to have the finest examples of life and learning presented to him in these formative years.

Radhakrishnan chose philosophy as the main subject in his BA degree course due to a very fortunate accident. At the time, he had been contemplating whether to choose from mathematics, physics, biology, philosophy and history, being interested in all five! By a happy coincidence, he happened to read at this time three well-known works on philosophy that a cousin, who had just then completed his degree in that subject, passed on to him. Radhakrishnan was so enamoured by this discovery of a subject that examined the nature of truth and of life, that he decided immediately on studying philosophy in greater depth. In addition to philosophy, Dr Radhakrishnan also studied Sanskrit and Hindi. He not only had great respect for the traditional languages of India, but a deep knowledge of the Vedas and Upanishads.

His career as a scholar, teacher, thinker and philosopher was long and distinguished, with him being associated with the most respected universities and institutions for many years.

After graduating with a Master's degree in philosophy from Madras Christian College, he occupied the King George V Chair of Mental and Moral Science at the University of Calcutta as a philosophy professor in 1921. During his tenure there, he represented the University of Calcutta at the Congress of the Universities of the British Empire in June 1926 and the International Congress of Philosophy at Harvard University in September 1926.

His services were next sought by Oxford University in 1929, when he was invited to take the post vacated by Principal J. Estlin Carpenter in Manchester College, Oxford. He lectured to students of Oxford University on comparative religion. In recognition of the high calibre of his knowledge and scholarship, a knighthood of the British Empire was conferred on him in 1931. From 1931 to 1936, he was appointed the vice-chancellor of Andhra University. In 1936 he returned to Oxford, becoming the Spalding Professor of Eastern religions and ethics at the university, and a Fellow of All Souls College.

After India's independence, another facet of Dr Radhakrishnan's abilities emerged when he represented India at UNESCO. His deft handling of this international appointment led to his becoming India's first ambassador in Moscow. His political career was also developing alongside. He had been an elected member of the Constituent Assembly of India – the organisation that was elected to write the Constitution of India, and which served as its first Parliament as an independent nation. After India became a republic in 1950, Dr Radhakrishnan was elected its first vice-president in 1952.

Some years after he suffered a personal setback with the death of his wife in 1956, Dr Radhakrishnan was elected to the post of president of the country and entered Rashtrapati Bhavan as the second president of independent India in 1962. He completed his term and handed over charge in 1967 to Zakir Husain. Cheered by his elevation to this august post, some of his friends and students wanted to celebrate his birthday in a grand style. In a characteristic manner, he asked instead that his birthday be celebrated as 'Teachers' Day', a tribute to those men and women who mould the character and minds of millions of children. This simple request reveals his innate humility and simplicity, and his ability to pursue an austere and unostentatious lifestyle even when showered with great recognition and rewards. Dr Radhakrishnan's wish was honoured, and ever since, Indians have celebrated 5 September as Teachers' Day.

In his writings, Dr Radhakrishnan pointed out that Western philosophers, despite all claims to objectivity, were influenced by the dominant beliefs of their own culture. His books on Indian philosophy matched those of the best scholars in the world, and were primarily responsible for Indian philosophy being taken seriously in the West. He proved the value of intuitive thinking as opposed to purely intellectual forms of thought. Indian readers know him best through his commentaries on the *Bhagavad Gita*, the Upanishads and the Brahma Sutra.

Among the host of recognitions bestowed on Dr Radhakrishnan were his becoming a Fellow of the British Academy in 1938, and the awarding of India's highest civilian award, the Bharat Ratna, to him in 1954, and the Order of Merit in 1963. He received the Peace Prize of the German Book Trade in 1961, and the Templeton

Prize in 1975, a few months before his death. The money from the Templeton Prize would be used to further scholarship, as Dr Radhakrishnan donated the entire amount to Oxford University. In memory of his distinguished scholarship, Oxford University instituted the Radhakrishnan Chevening Scholarships and the Radhakrishnan Memorial Award.

This gentle philosopher had many friends and admirers. Paying tribute to him, Jawaharlal Nehru said, 'He has served his country in many capacities. But above all, he is a great teacher from whom all of us have learnt much and will continue to learn. It is India's peculiar privilege to have a great philosopher, a great educationist and a great humanist as her president. That in itself shows the kind of men we honour and respect.'

Zakir Husain (1897–1969)

Aristocrat and Educationist
Zakir Husain

Term of Office: 13 May 1967–3 May 1969

One among the two Indian presidents who have tragically died in office before completing their term, Dr Zakir Husain was the third president of the Republic of India. Born in Hyderabad on 8 February 1897, he belonged to an upper middle-class Pathan family from Qaunganj in the Farrukhabad district of Uttar Pradesh. His father, Fida Hussain Khan, had moved to Hyderabad, where he had a very successful legal career. His early death, when Hussain was only ten years old, was a blow to the future president.

First sent to be educated at the Islamia High School in Etawah, Uttar Pradesh, Hussain received instruction in the scriptures of his religion, Islam. His higher education was at Aligarh at the Muhammadan Anglo Oriental College, where he completed his MA degree.

He was twenty-three years old when the Indian National Congress and the All India Khilafat Committee joined hands in launching the Non-Cooperation Movement. Mahatma Gandhi was then touring the country to convince teachers and students to leave government-administered schools and colleges as part of the protest against the British. Young Zakir Husain was by then half-student and half-teacher, and very popular among both students and staff. At his persuasion, Hakim Ajmal Khan and other leaders came together to establish the Jamia Millia Islamia, a national educational institution, at Aligarh on 29 October, 1920. This was no mean achievement. The Jamia Millia Islamia went on to have great significance during the freedom struggle and was a centre for young nationalists as well as liberal and enlightened thought within Islam.

However, Zakir Husain was not content to rest on his laurels for having helped to create such a fine institution. Feeling the need to study further, he joined the University of Berlin in Germany in

1923 and returned with a doctorate in economics three years later. He then rejoined the Jamia Millia in March 1926 and became its shaikhu jamia or vice-chancellor. It was in the evolution and nurturing of Jamia Millia that Hussain really came into his own as an educationist. This experience and his deep understanding of the basic philosophy of education was what led to his taking charge of the Basic National Education scheme when it was launched in 1938. From 1938 to 1948, he was the president of the Hindustani Talimi Sangh, Sevagram, an organisation dedicated to furthering the education of Indian Muslims.

Continuing his service to the cause of education, Hussain was appointed vice-chancellor of Aligarh Muslim University in November 1948. This was considered a very significant appointment. Aligarh Muslim University – previously MAO College, Hussain's alma mater – was then under the dominant influence of the Muslim League. Their ideas of a separate nation-state for Muslims were attracting a sizeable section of the students. This was one of the reasons why some nationalist Muslims decided to establish the Jamia Millia Islamia. In fact, their different approaches to the education and representation of Indian Muslims were what caused Dr Zakir Husain to become a political opponent of Muslim League leader Mohammed Ali Jinnah. Dr Zakir Husain believed that the future of Indian Muslims was inextricably tied to the future of India, while Jinnah took the road that ultimately resulted in the Partition. Dr. Hussain therefore, took over as vice-chancellor at a time when Aligarh Muslim University was struggling to recover from its association with the Muslim League, and when even speaking in Urdu was seen to be a sign of a traitor. Dr Zakir Husain, however, was determined to protect the place of Urdu in the educational, social and cultural life of India. He collected more than 22 lakh signatures from Muslims, asking for Urdu to be accorded the status of an Indian language, with a recognised history and literature. This helped pull the community out of the guilt and depression they had sunk into, to join the national mainstream. After Partition, it was left to leaders like Maulana Azad and Dr Zakir Husain to truly represent their community and do whatever they could to alleviate the problems of Indian Muslims as the citizens of a free India.

The next few years saw Dr Hussain nominated to a number of important appointments such as the membership of the Indian Universities Commission, chairman of the Indian National Committee at the World University Service, and its world president in 1954, Indian representative on the executive board of UNESCO from 1956 to 1958, and Rajya Sabha membership.

Continuously involved with the cause of education, he remained the chairman of the Central Board of Secondary Education till 1957, a member of the University Grants Commission till 1957, a member of the University Education Commission from 1948 to 1949 and of the Educational Reorganisation Committee of Bihar, Uttar Pradesh and Madhya Pradesh. His election to the highest office of the land was preceded by five years as the governor of Bihar from 1957 to 1962.

He was declared elected and sworn in as the third President of the Indian Republic in 1962. His sudden death on 3 May 1969 while still in office was a tragic loss to the nation.

Dr Zakir Husain was decorated with the Padma Vibhushan in 1954 and received the Bharat Ratna, India's highest civilian honour, in 1963. He received a number of honorary D.Litt degrees by the universities of Delhi, Calcutta, Aligarh, Allahabad and Cairo.

A scholarly and refined individual who embodied the qualities of unfailing politeness, culture and taste, Dr Zakir Husain translated Plato's *Republic* and Edward Cannan's *Elementary Political Economy* into Urdu soon after joining the Jamia Millia in 1920. While studying at Berlin, he got an edition of the *Diwan-I-Ghalib*, the works of noted Urdu poet Ghalib, printed. He painstakingly did much of the composition himself, because the press did not have enough staff. Another book he brought out at this time was one in German on Mahatma Gandhi (*Die Botschaft des Mahatma Gandhi* – 'The Message of Mahatma Gandhi'). He excelled in writing for children and wrote stories notable for their style and craft.

An imposing personality because of his tall and well-built stature, Dr Zakir Husain gave evidence of an aristocratic upbringing in the wide range of interests he had cultivated. Sensitive to beauty and art, he had a number of hobbies such as the collection of cacti, fossils, paintings, specimens of calligraphy and objets d'art, and a rich and magnificent library. He wore his religion lightly – like the Sufis, his religion was never obvious, although he was a deeply spiritual man. As for his nationalist ideals, they derived from the highest moral values. In his inaugural speech, he declared that the whole of India was his home and all its people were his family, a statement that truly sums up his work and life.

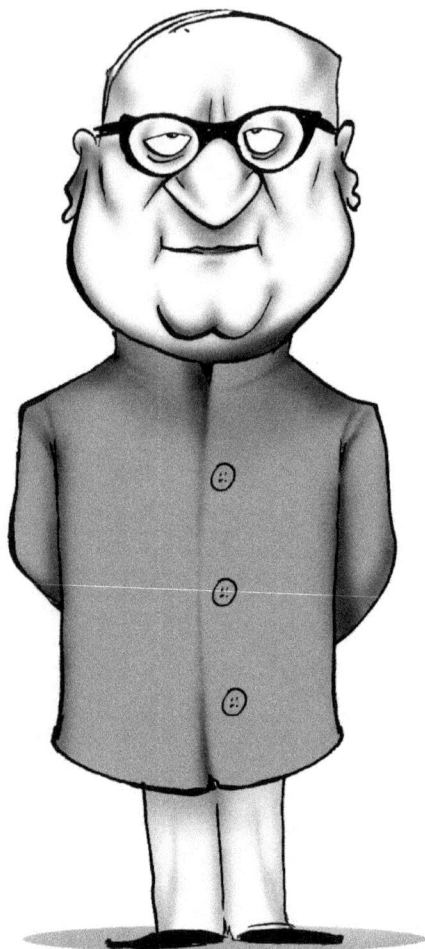

Varahagiri Venkata Giri (1894–1980)

Trade Unionist President
Varahagiri Venkata Giri

Term of Office: 3 May 1969–20 July 1969; 24 August 1969–24 August 1974

The sedate and imposing environment of Rashtrapati Bhavan is a far cry from the rough and tumble of trade union rallies, public meetings and slogans of workers' solidarity. Yet for one president of the Indian republic, this path of public participation was the route that led to his becoming the head of the Indian State. This was Varahagiri Venkata Giri, or V.V. Giri as he was widely known.

Born on 10 August 1894 at Berhampore in Ganjam district of Orissa, which was then a part of the Madras Presidency, Giri came from a well-off family of Telugu-speaking Brahmins.

His father, V.V. Jogaiah Pantulu, was a prominent lawyer and head of the local Bar association. Like many others in the legal profession, he was also keenly interested in the struggle for Indian independence, and had joined the Swarajya party founded by Pandit Motilal Nehru and Chittaranjan Das in the 1920s. He was a member of the Central Legislative Assembly from 1927 to 1930, and was elected to the Madras Legislative Council after the introduction of the Government of India Act of 1935.

Apart from his legal profession, Giri's father Jogaiah took an active interest in the Bengal Nagpur Railway Workers' Union. The lively atmosphere in Giri's parental home, permeated by the freedom struggle and the railway workers' union activities, was a strong influence on him in the years he was growing up. At an early age, Giri was married to Saraswati Bai. While his formative education was in his home town, in 1913 he left the country to study law at University College in Dublin. Here he came in close contact with leaders of the Irish nationalist movement Sinn Fein. Giri was fired by the ideas of Eamon de Valera, Michael Collins, Patrick Pearse, Desmond FitzGerald, Eoin MacNeil, James Connolly and others. His involvement with these Irish revolutionaries led to his being expelled from Ireland in 1916. He returned to India and was called to the Bar to become a practising lawyer.

By this time Giri had not only evolved into a militant nationalist but also a lawyer who was committed to serving the interests of working people. He had learnt much from the Irish trade union movement. On his return to his home town, he started his legal practice and simultaneously plunged into the nationalist movement. He was a part of the Home Rule League and a member of the Indian National Congress. As a young freedom fighter who joined Mahatma Gandhi's Non-Cooperation Movement without a thought for the lucrative professional practice he was putting aside, Giri was arrested and imprisoned for some time.

From 1922 Giri's energies would be directed exclusively towards the organisation of the working classes. It was in this year that he became associated with N.M. Joshi, who is considered largely responsible for building the trade union movement. The movement absorbed and sustained Giri. He was always proud of being a trade unionist and considered his close ties with workers as being the main source of his strength. The decade of the twenties saw him rise from strength to strength within the workers' movement. He was one of the founders of the All India Railwaymen's Federation in 1923, and twice elected president of the Trade Union Congress, in 1926 and 1942. He began attending many international gatherings as a leading trade unionist. Some notable occasions were the International Labour Conference at Geneva in 1927, as well as the Trade Union Congress at the same venue. In 1931–32 he was the workers' representative in London for the Second Round Table Conference.

The Civil Disobedience Movement launched by Mahatma Gandhi in the early thirties gave Giri an opportunity to use his wide-ranging influence among trade unions. He organised these active and aware groups to join the mainstream movement for Indian independence. From 1934 to 1937, V.V. Giri was a member of the Indian Legislative Assembly, where he managed to hold his own in a House which had illustrious orators and legislators such as Satyamurty, Bhulabhai Desai, Mohammed Ali Jinnah, Govind Ballabh Pant, Madan Mohan Malaviya, Asaf Ali and others. In this Assembly, Giri began to be known as a significant and persuasive speaker on labour issues.

After the introduction of the Government of India Act of 1935, the last pre-independence Constitution drafted by the British, general elections were held in 1936. Giri fought the election on a Congress ticket in Madras, against the raja of Bobbili, who was then the most powerful political personality in the Madras Presidency. The raja of Bobbili, leader of the Justice party and the chief minister of the province, looked upon the constituency as a family fiefdom since his family had always enjoyed clout among the people there. Giri's chances against such a powerful candidate were considered slim; it was as if an ant was challenging an elephant. However, in this showdown between a feudal leader and a popular leader Giri emerged victorious, ushering in a new era in the political history of the region. His historic win meant that Giri was taken into the Cabinet of the C. Rajagopalachari Congress ministry in Madras in 1937 where he was given the portfolio of Labour. He was re-elected in the general elections of 1946, and he was once again given the portfolio of Labour in the Cabinet formed by T. Prakasam. His next assignment was as India's High Commissioner in Ceylon, as Sri Lanka was then known.

The years 1952 to 1957 marked Giri's presence in the Lok Sabha. In this period he was a member of the Union Cabinet from 1952 to 1954 with the Labour portfolio. In an act that seems remarkable today, when politicians do anything to hold on to their posts of office, he resigned from the Union Cabinet when he differed with the government on a particular labour issue. However, as if to emphasise the justice of his stand, the government eventually came round to what he had been trying to say all along.

Having completed his Lok Sabha term, Giri began to serve as governor in various states such as Uttar Pradesh, Kerala and Mysore, where he was successively posted after 1957. His dynamic personality ensured his popularity everywhere he went. Most importantly, he served as a mentor for the younger generation of leaders and activists, and initiated new directions and activities in the field of social work. He was elected to the office of president of the Indian Conference of Social Work in 1958.

In 1967, he was appointed to the post of vice-president of the country, and was thrust into the

presidential chair for the first time when President
Dr Zakir Husain passed away in office on 3 May
1969. Having officiated as the president during
this period, V.V. Giri was so confident about his
election to the post that he offered himself as a
candidate for the following presidential election
without going through the procedure of garnering
support from political parties. In his mind and
heart, he knew that he was the popular choice of
the people for president. Giri won the presidential
election of 1969 and became the fourth president
of the Republic of India with the overwhelming
support of the people's representatives that elect
the president. As this trade unionist champion
of workers entered the Rashtrapati Bhavan, the
presidential post was freed from the preserve of
politicians and became a reflection of the common
man and citizen.

Typically, the two important books that Giri
authored were *Industrial Relations* and *Labour
Problems in Indian Industry.* From his idealistic
youth, right up to the end, Giri was a committed
socialist, but his socialism was of the kind that
was not bookish or theoretical but connected
in the most practical of ways with the lives of
the common people. He remained president till

1974, and in 1975, this irrepressible leader of the workers was awarded the Bharat Ratna, India's highest civilian honour.

Fakhruddin Ali Ahmed (1905–1977)

'Emergency President'
Fakhruddin Ali Ahmed

Term of Office: 24 August 1974–11 February 1977

D
r Fakhruddin Ali Ahmed was the president who proclaimed the two-year period of Emergency that marked such a difficult period in India's political history. This, and his subsequent death in office, marked him in public memory forever as the 'Emergency President'.

The fifth president of the Republic of India, Fakhruddin Ali Ahmed was born on 13 May 1905 in Delhi, into a well-off family. His grandfather was Khaliluddin Ali Ahmed, originally from Kacharighat near Golaghat town in the Sibsagar district of Assam. Khaliluddin's wife, Fakhruddin's grandmother, came from one of the families who were part of Emperor Aurangzeb's bid to conquer Assam. Moving in the highest social circles of those days, Fakhruddin's father, Col. Zalnur Ali, showed spirit and resistance to the British in an incident that led to his being banished to the distant Northwest province of the British Raj. Col. Zalnur Ali was an officer of the Indian Medical Service. When he was a bachelor doctor posted at Shillong, Col. Ali and one of his colleagues, Col. Sibram Bora, were allotted seats placed away from the European guests at a function in the Shillong Club. Enraged at this social segregation, the two Assamese colonels boycotted the function in protest. This show of resistance was enough to anger his European bosses who transferred Col. Zalnur Ali to the Northwest province. It was here that he came in contact with the Nawab of Lohari in Delhi, whose daughter he married. Fakhruddin Ali Ahmed was born here, where his maternal grandfather lived.

Fakhruddin first went to school at the Bonda Government High School in Uttar Pradesh, later matriculating from the Delhi Government High School, then under the Punjab University. Like many of his contemporaries from well-off families, he was sent to England for higher education in

1923. His parents wanted him to serve later as an officer of the Indian Civil Service. While his mother wanted the best for her son, she was against his being sent abroad. However, Fakhruddin's father's will prevailed.

Fakhruddin studied at Cambridge University's Catherine College and became a barrister from the Inner Temple of London. He could not complete his parents' dream of appearing for the ICS examination due to a severe bout of illness. When he returned to India, he began practising law in the Lahore high court in 1928. In October that year, his father took him to Guwahati in Assam to take care of some matters relating to his paternal property, which included a few hundred acres of land in and around Guwahati.

Thus the Ahmed family connection to Assam, which had been abruptly severed by Fakhruddin's father's posting to the northwest many years ago, was restored, and two years later, when Fakhruddin Ali Ahmed revisited Guwahati, he came in contact with the leaders of the Congress in Assam. In 1931 he enrolled as a primary member of the Congress, a move that would greatly influence his future development.

As a student in England, Ali Ahmed had met Jawaharlal Nehru, whose progressive ideas had made a deep impression on him. From the 1930s, Nehru became a close friend and mentor. After Ali Ahmed had joined the Indian National Congress, he stayed steadfastly as a member, following its policies although fellow Muslims tried to get him to leave the party and join the Muslim League instead.

Being a part of the freedom struggle led by the Congress, Ali Ahmed protested with individual 'satyagraha' on 14 December 1940, for which he was imprisoned for a year. He was arrested again on 9 August 1942 when he was returning after attending the historic session of the All India Congress Committee at Bombay that launched the Quit India Movement, and was detained for three-and-a-half years till April 1945.

It was during this period that Ali Ahmed entered into matrimony with Abida, who had studied in Aligarh Muslim University. When this match was being negotiated, Ali Ahmed was undergoing a jail term in Jorhat. This led to the piquant situation where, when Abida's family wanted to know what the prospective bridegroom was doing, the answer that came from one of Ali Ahmed's relatives was 'Fil hal to jail mein hain' (Well, right now he is in jail)! Despite such hiccups, however, Ali Ahmed and Abida were married on 9 November 1945. Later, Begum Abida Saheba also enjoyed a brief political career, being elected to the Lok Sabha from Uttar Pradesh in 1981, in a by-election.

Within the Congress party, Ali Ahmed held several important organisational positions. He was a member of the Assam Pradesh Congress Committee from 1936 right up to the 1970s. He was elected to the Assam Assembly for the first time in 1935 and became the minister of Finance, Revenue and Labour in the Congress coalition ministry formed by Gopinath Bardoloi on 19 September 1938. From his very first term as minister, Ali Ahmed showed remarkable administrative ability. He was responsible for introducing the Assam Agricultural Income Tax Bill, which was the first of its kind in India. This law levied taxes on tea garden lands in Assam.

When workers in the British-owned Assam Oil Company Ltd at Digboi went on strike, Ali Ahmed's pro-labour measures angered the Europeans and their agents, who saw the actions of the Congress coalition government as hostile to the interests of the British commercial community. Unfazed by such opposition, Ali Ahmed went ahead with the measures, which won him and the Bardoloi ministry a great deal of popularity. In late 1939 the Bardoloi ministry had to resign because of differences with the British government regarding India's participation in the Second World War. By this time however, Ali Ahmed had established himself as an able administrator.

Following Independence, Ali Ahmed's political career continued in Assam, where he was elected on the Congress ticket to the Assam Assembly in 1957 and 1962. He had also been a member of the Rajya Sabha before this, from 1952 to 1953, and served as the advocate-general of the Government of Assam. Ali Ahmed was a senior minister in the B.P. Chaliha-led government in Assam from 1957 till Nehru called him to join his Cabinet at the Centre in January 1966. This signalled the beginning of his work at the Centre.

Ali Ahmed fought and won the Lok Sabha elections in 1971 from the Barpeta constituency. While Nehru was prime minister, Ali Ahmed was given important portfolios in the Cabinet, such as Food and Agriculture, Cooperation, Education, Industrial Development and Company Laws. As a loyal friend of Nehru and a proven administrator, such key assignments were quite natural. Within the Congress party, Ali Ahmed enjoyed considerable clout as a member of the Congress Working Committee for several years.

In 1969, some years after the death of Nehru, the Congress party split. During this division between loyalists to the Nehru-Gandhi family and other leaders like Morarji Desai, Ali Ahmed remained with Indira Gandhi. In fact, his long and close association with the Nehru family may have been the factor that made him accept Indira Gandhi's leadership till his death.

Ali Ahmed was elected president of the Indian Republic on 29 August 1974. He put his signature as president to the order on promulgation of Emergency on 25 June 1975 – the most notable decision of his presidential term. This move was widely criticised by Opposition leaders, who considered it a servile act, driven more by considerations of being seen as loyal to the Nehru-Gandhi family, rather than of genuine concern for the safety of the country. The proclamation of the Emergency, a move recommended by then prime minister Indira Gandhi, endowed her with sweeping powers and led to the jailing of all her political opponents in the name of national security.

Perhaps the widespread criticism of his capitulation to Indira Gandhi affected Ali Ahmed more than he ever showed. He died of a sudden heart attack on 11 February 1977 in the Rashtrapati Bhavan. He had returned from a tour of the Southeast Asian countries only a day before. When Ali Ahmed passed away he left behind his wife, two sons and a daughter. Emergency was later revoked, on 21 March 1977.

A gentleman president from the upper strata of society, Ali Ahmed's upbringing seldom allowed anger and prejudices to get the better of him. He was also a staunch Congressman, with a deep commitment to secularism. That his calm and patriotic demeanour ruffled those whose outlook was narrow and communal can be illustrated by a well-known incident which occurred in 1935. At this time, Mohammad Ali Jinnah, Liaquat Ali Khan, Nazimuddin and a few other stalwarts of the Muslim League came to Assam to campaign against Ali Ahmed. The future president had been pitted by the Congress against a Muslim League candidate in the Assembly polls. At this time, a common friend suggested that Ali Ahmed should pay a courtesy call to the Muslim League leaders staying at Guwahati. Liaquat Ali angrily rebuffed this suggestion saying that he would not shake hands with a 'kafir' or unbeliever, meaning Ali Ahmed. The meeting with the Muslim League leaders never took place. Unfortunately, later in life, Ali Ahmed had to contend with being called 'communal' because he tried to attract young Muslims who had been educated at Aligarh Muslim University – a campus then perceived to be influenced by the communal ideas of the Muslim League – to the Congress.

A man with many interests and activities, Ali Ahmed was an avid tennis player and golfer. He was elected president of the Assam Football Association and the Assam Cricket Association for several terms, and also served as the vice-president of the Assam Sports Council. He was elected president of the All India Cricket Association in 1967, and was an active member of the Delhi Golf Club and the Delhi Gymkhana Club from 1961. Endowed with a deep respect for music and the fine arts, he immersed himself in the poetical works of Ghalib.

He was awarded an honorary doctorate by the University of Pristina, Kosovo, in 1975, during his visit to Yugoslavia. Sophisticated and well-travelled, Ali Ahmed will be remembered for his urbane worldview, apart from his inevitable connection to the Emergency.

Neelam Sanjiva Reddy (1913–1996)

Consensus Choice for President
Neelam Sanjiva Reddy

Term of Office: 25 July 1977–25 July 1982

The bickering among political parties of different ideologies and interests is a familiar aspect of public life in India. Such differences become more pronounced on the eve of an election for the post of president of India. Elected through a system of electoral colleges consisting of MPs and MLAs, the post of president becomes a test of the relative clout of different political camps. This has been the scenario in recent times.

However, one president was unanimously selected as the consensus candidate for the post of president by all political parties, and declared elected unopposed on 21 July 1977. He was Neelam Sanjiva Reddy, the sixth president of India.

Neelam Sanjiva Reddy was born on 18 May 1913 into a peasant family in Illuru village in Anantapur district of Andhra Pradesh. He attended school in Chennai, then known as Madras, studying at the Theosophical High School at Adyar. Later he went on to study at the Arts College in Anantapur.

In July 1929 Mahatma Gandhi visited Anantapur — a turning point for the young and idealistic Reddy. Profoundly influenced by Gandhiji's thoughts, words and actions, he decided to wear khadi and discard British-made clothes and goods. Now determined to study in the school of life, rather than in the confines of an educational institution, Reddy gave up his studies and joined the freedom struggle. He joined the Congress party in 1931.

The next few years were full of nationalist activities for Reddy, who was a part of the Youth League and participated in student satyagraha demonstrations. He began to be noticed for his organisational and oratorical skills, and was elected to the post of secretary of the Andhra Pradesh Provincial Congress Committee at the age of twenty-five.

Reddy's marriage to Nagarathnamma took place on 8 June 1935. The couple went on to have a son and three daughters.

His involvement in the freedom struggle led to Reddy's imprisonment for the most part of the years from 1940 to 1945. When he was imprisoned in Amravati jail in 1942, his jail mates were his political colleagues and contemporaries such as K. Kamaraj, Satyamurti and T. Prakasam, all Congress leaders from Tamil Nadu, and V.V. Giri, then imprisoned for his role in the Quit India Movement.

An active Congressman, Reddy fought elections and was elected to the Madras Legislative Assembly in 1946. In 1947, he became the secretary of the Madras Congress Legislature Party, and, most importantly, a member of the Indian Constituent Assembly.

Reddy was part of the government of the composite state of Madras from April 1949 to April 1951, when he was minister for Prohibition, Housing and Forests. In 1951 he resigned this office to contest for the post of president of the Andhra Pradesh Congress Committee. That same year his five-year-old son died in a motor accident. Completely devastated by the tragedy,

Reddy resigned as APCC president. It was only the persistent efforts of the rank and file of the party that persuaded him to withdraw his resignation some time later.

The next two decades of the fifties and sixties saw Reddy gather valuable experience as an administrator. He was elected a Rajya Sabha member in 1952, and served as deputy chief minister in the Cabinet of T. Prakasam in 1953, as well as the Cabinet of B. Gopala Reddi in 1955.

When the new state of Andhra Pradesh was formed in October 1956, Reddy became its first chief minister. He briefly relinquished this post to take over as the president of the Indian National Congress in 1959. He became chief minister again in 1962, but in 1964, although he was re-elected as the leader of the Congress Legislature Party, he recommended the name of his colleague K. Brahmananda Reddy to the governor to be invited to form the ministry.

June 1964 saw the entry of Reddy into the Union Cabinet of Prime Minister Lal Bahadur Shastri, when he was appointed minister for Steel and Mines. He was elected to the Rajya Sabha in November 1964.

In 1966, when Indira Gandhi became prime minister, Reddy joined her government as Union minister of Transport, Civil Aviation, Shipping and Tourism. He fought the general elections of 1967, and was elected from the Hindupur constituency in Andhra Pradesh. He was elected Speaker in the new Lok Sabha on 17 March 1967. Reddy conducted the business of Parliament so smoothly and efficiently that he won acclaim and admiration from leaders of all political parties.

Reddy's long association with the Congress, the party that had been associated with the Indian freedom struggle, came to an end in regrettable circumstances. He resigned from the post of Speaker of the Lok Sabha on 19 July 1969 to contest the presidential election as a nominee of the Congress. His nomination had been filed by Indira Gandhi. However, after filing his nomination, Indira Gandhi subsequently organised his defeat in the elections by unethical means, possibly because she felt that Reddy may not always be amenable to her way of approaching and solving issues. Disillusioned with the Congress and its cult of the politics of personality, Reddy parted ways with the party and Indira Gandhi.

For some years after 1969 Reddy removed himself from the political arena, going back to agriculture, which had always remained a passion with him. He emerged from this self-imposed political seclusion on 1 May 1975 by addressing a public meeting in Hyderabad along with freedom fighter and political leader Jayaprakash Narayan. This signalled the beginning of his association with the Opposition parties. He fought elections in March 1977 as a Janata party candidate from the Nandyal constituency in Andhra Pradesh and was the only non-Congress candidate to get elected from the state.

Reddy became Speaker of the Lok Sabha for the second time on 26 March 1977. Like the previous occasion, he resigned from office two years later to file his nomination for the post of president of India in July 1977. This time, however, there was a vital difference. Winning the support of all political parties and emerging as the single consensus candidate, Neelam Sanjiva Reddy was declared elected unopposed on 21 July 1977 to become the sixth President of our country.

Reddy's elevation to this post marked his evolution from being a staunch Congressman to becoming a Janata party leader. In some ways this mirrored India's own political evolution — from being a country dominated by a single party to being a democracy with room for multiple parties and ideologies.

Giani Zail Singh (1916–1994)

A Scholar and a Rebel
Giani Zail Singh

Term of Office: 25 July 1982–25 July 1987

Being able to stand up to injustice throughout one's life, in the midst of great social change and upheaval, requires a robust and unconquerable spirit. One president of modern India had such spirit in ample measure. In his lifetime, he challenged feudal princely power and foreign domination, and fought against communalism and social injustice. He was recognised as a learned and aristocratic personality, but was also someone who was completely unassuming and a friend of the poor and downtrodden. The man who successfully combined all these exceptional qualities was Giani Zail Singh, the seventh president of the Republic of India.

Giani Zail Singh, one of three sons of Sardar Kishan Singh, a farmer, was born on 5 May 1916 in a mud house in Sandhwan village of Faridkot district. His humble origins as well as his family's background of being artisans in previous generations meant that Zail Singh grew up with a healthy respect for work done with one's hands. He learnt to stitch clothes, crush stones, plough fields, lay roads and dig wells, understanding the needs and aspirations of the common man like few others have done in childhood. His basic education included studying the *Koran*, *Bhagavad Gita* and *Ramayana* besides the Sikh scriptures.

Showing a pronounced thirst for knowledge uncommon in boys of his age, Zail Singh had completed the study of Sikh religion, Sikh history and Sikh scriptures by the age when most complete only their school education. This earned him the respectful honorific title of 'Giani', or scholar. He was fluent in Hindi and Urdu, although not as comfortable in English. Zail Singh's entire personality commanded respect by its example of self-reliance and resolute determination, enabling him to carve a solid reputation for himself in public life.

Zail Singh's earliest inspiration came from the martyrdom of Bhagat Singh and his companions on 23 March 1931. The young Giani, then only sixteen, was very much moved. Some years later, in 1938, he set up a branch of the All India Congress in the state of Faridkot. This was then a princely state, and its ruler, the maharaja, crushed any sign of revolt against the British. Because of his attempts to bring the Congress to Faridkot, Zail Singh was proclaimed and treated as an ordinary criminal. He was sentenced to five years in solitary confinement – a form of punishment that could have broken a lesser man. His crime: founding the office of the Congress in Faridkot to spearhead the freedom struggle.

When he was released after five years, he spent some time outside the state because of continued harassment by the maharaja's administration. Typically, he used this time to canvass support for the freedom movement among the people. At the same time, he came under the influence of Mahatma Gandhi and his message of non-violence.

Zail Singh returned to Faridkot in 1946 to resume the struggle for independence – this time on the lines indicated by Mahatma Gandhi.

One of the first issues that united the people of Faridkot was the question of raising the national flag. The maharaja responded with such a wave of violence and terror against the people that Jawaharlal Nehru himself decided to visit Faridkot to hoist the tricolour. This was the beginning of the relationship shared by Giani Zail Singh and Nehru, after which they stayed in close contact, with Nehru keeping a kind and encouraging eye on the young freedom fighter.

A very dramatic moment in Zail Singh's life was when he was held guilty of leading a revolt against the maharaja of Faridkot and setting up a parallel government. He was arrested by the raja's men, bound hand and foot and tied to a Jeep. He was then threatened with being dragged around the streets of Faridkot if he did not mend his ways. While Zail Singh himself stood firm, the people's response to their tyrannical actions made the guards abandon their mission.

Zail Singh's administrative experience began when the kingdom of Faridkot was merged with the state of Patiala and East Punjab States Union or PEPSU. He became minister for Revenue and Agriculture in this new consolidated state and worked tirelessly to remove the socio-economic injustice faced by farm labourers, small cultivators and tenants. Abolition of absentee landlordism and proprietary rights belonging to the actual tillers of the land were two revolutionary steps he initiated, as well as legislative measures ensuring the security of tenancy and the rights of tenants to share lands which had been declared as 'surplus' after the application of land-ceiling. In fact, these agrarian reforms were later emulated by other states and gave great credit to Zail Singh's far-sightedness and sense of justice.

By November 1956 PEPSU was integrated with the state of Punjab, marking a new phase in Zail Singh's public life. He became a member of the Rajya Sabha and led the Punjab Pradesh Congress Committee as senior vice-president. In these roles he worked hard to inspire his party men and ensure their victories in the 1962 general elections to both the Punjab Vidhan Sabha and the Lok Sabha. When the Pratap Singh Kairon government was sworn in at the state level, Zail Singh was made a minister, but he resigned his office in order to work at the grassroots level following the difficult period faced by the country after the war with China.

For the next ten years, from 1962 to 1972, Zail Singh worked to defeat the forces of communalism and exploitation in Punjab. It was his staunch and steadfast leadership as president of the Punjab Pradesh Congress Committee that kept the rank and file of the party together and enabled the decisive and overwhelming majority for the Congress in the 1971 Lok Sabha elections and the 1972 Punjab elections.

Inevitably and deservedly, Zail Singh was elected unanimously by the Punjab Congress Legislative Party to be the chief minister of Punjab in March 1972. During his term Punjab made enviable strides in industrialisation and agriculture, with the Green Revolution. Also, most importantly, under a man well-versed in faith and committed to secularism, Punjab remained a peaceful state with harmony among people from all faiths.

As chief minister of Punjab, Zail Singh derived strength from the leadership of Indira Gandhi. His closeness to this political icon of India, who was nearly always surrounded by controversy, led to a series of difficulties and embarrassments for him after 1977, when the first Janata party or non-Congress government came to power at the Centre. Taking such opposition in his stride, Zail Singh once more plunged into the rough and tumble of the general elections in 1980, winning from Hoshiarpur constituency with a comprehensive lead of over 125,000 votes over his nearest rival to enter the seventh Lok Sabha. Indira Gandhi rewarded him with the key portfolio of the Home ministry in her Cabinet.

Zail Singh's most notable contribution as Home minister was the way he handled the Assam agitation, bringing its key players to the negotiating table, and the way he dealt firmly with communal riots in any part of the country. He was undoubtedly able to make such a good impact as Home minister because of his innate lack of malice and sense of fair play when handling differing viewpoints and faiths.

In July 1982 Zail Singh was elected to the highest office of the country: president. It was indeed tragic that he was the president of India when the 1984 anti-Sikh riots took place in New Delhi and other parts of the country. The latter part of his term was fuelled by rumours of his strained relationship with Rajiv Gandhi, who succeeded Indira Gandhi as prime minister. However, being the thorough gentleman that he was, he declined to embarrass the Congress government headed by Rajiv, by seeking re-election as president of India with the support of non-Congress parties.

Zail Singh died in a road accident on 25 December 1994, near Kiratpur Sahib in Ropar district. With his death, the curtain came down on one of the most remarkable personalities of modern India, each chapter of whose life mirrored the social, political and economic changes in our history.

R. Venkataraman (1910–2009)

Legal Luminary President
R. Venkataraman

Term of Office: 25 July 1987–25 July 1992

A grasp of the intricacies of law is practically a must for those interested in a career in politics. R. Venkataraman, the eighth president of the Republic of India, exemplified this command over the law and legal matters. He was born on 4 December 1910 in the village of Rajamadam, near Pattukottai town of Thanjavur district in Tamil Nadu.

Venkataraman studied at local schools before going to the city of Madras, now known as Chennai, for his higher education. Here he first got his Master's degree in economics, and later qualified in law from Law College. Venkataraman enrolled as a lawyer in the high court, Madras in 1935.

The year 1938 marked Venkataraman's entry into the life of a householder, with his marriage to Janaki Venkataraman. The couple was blessed with three daughters. Now a practising lawyer, Venkataraman was drawn into the movement for India's freedom. He plunged wholeheartedly into the Quit India Movement of 1942, and was imprisoned for two years.

From an early stage of his legal career, Venkataraman showed a keen interest in the law as it applied to labour. When he was released from prison in 1944, he took up the task of organising the labour section of the Tamil Nadu Provincial Congress Committee. In 1949 his deep knowledge and interest led him to begin the *Labour Law Journal*, which publishes landmark judgements and new laws relating to labour. This specialist publication is widely respected by lawyers and trade unionists alike. Through his practice and organisational work, Venkataraman came in intimate contact with trade union workers. He founded and led several unions in this period, such as the unions for plantation workers, estate staff, dock workers, railway workers and working journalists.

His skills as a lawyer had earned Venkataraman a strong reputation among his peers and the legal establishment. In 1946, he was sent to Malaysia and Singapore by the Government of India, when the transfer of power from British to Indian hands was imminent. He was one of a panel of lawyers sent to defend Indian nationals charged with offences during the Japanese occupation of those two places. From 1947 to 1950, Venkataraman served as secretary of the Madras Provincial Bar Federation. He was called to the Supreme Court in 1951.

A political career was inevitable with Venkataraman's increased participation in trade union activity. He was a member of the Constituent Assembly that drafted India's Constitution. He was elected first in 1950, to free India's Provisional Parliament and later to the first Parliament, whose term ran from 1952 to1957. As a parliamentarian, Venkataraman went to attend the 1952 Session of the Metal Trades Committee of the International Labour Organisation as a workers' delegate. He also held office within the ranks of the Congress party, becoming the secretary of the Congress Parliamentary Party from 1953 to 1954.

A fresh direction to his political career emerged in 1957, when Venkataraman, re-elected to Parliament, chose to resign from his seat in the Lok Sabha to join the state government of Madras as a minister. For the next ten years, till 1967, he continued as a minister in the state government with different portfolios such as Industries, Labour, Cooperation, Power, Transport and Commercial Taxes. This ministerial stint also saw him being the leader of the Madras Legislative Council.

By 1967 Venkataraman had moved to Delhi where he was appointed a member of the Union Planning Commission in 1967, entrusted with Industry, Labour, Power, Transport, Communications and Railways. He served in this office till 1971. In 1977, when there was an anti-Congress wave sweeping the country in the general elections, Venkataraman was elected on a Congress ticket to the Lok Sabha from the Madras (South) Constituency. In the stormy days of the Janata government at the Centre following the 1977 elections, he was an active Opposition Member of Parliament and chairman of the Public Accounts Committee.

Called to represent India at several international forums, Venkataraman was governor of the

International Monetary Fund, the International Bank for Reconstruction and Development, and the Asian Development Bank at different periods. He was an Indian delegate to the United Nations General Assembly in 1953, 1955, 1956, 1958, 1959, 1960 and 1961. He led the Indian delegation to the 42nd Session of the International Labour Conference at Geneva in 1958 and represented India in the Inter Parliamentary Conference in Vienna in 1978. He was a member of the United Nations Administrative Tribunal from 1955 to 1979 and was its president from 1968 to 1979.

Venkataraman's path to Rashtrapati Bhavan saw him becoming the Union minister of Finance in the government headed by Indira Gandhi in 1980, after being re-elected to the Lok Sabha. He was later entrusted with the key portfolio of Defence. Serving in these important ministerial posts as Union minister made Venkataraman a strong candidate for vice-president of India and then its eighth president.

A soft-spoken man with a gentle sense of humour, who evolved from a fiery labour lawyer to a politically wise and experienced president, Venkataraman received a number of honorary degrees and awards. He received an honorary

Doctorate of Law from his alma mater, the University of Madras, besides similar honours from Nagarjuna University, Madras Medical College, University of Roorkee and the University of Burdwan. He was awarded the Tamra Patra for participation in the freedom struggle. The Shankaracharya of Kancheepuram bestowed the title of 'Sat Seva Ratna' on R. Venkataraman for his service to the country.

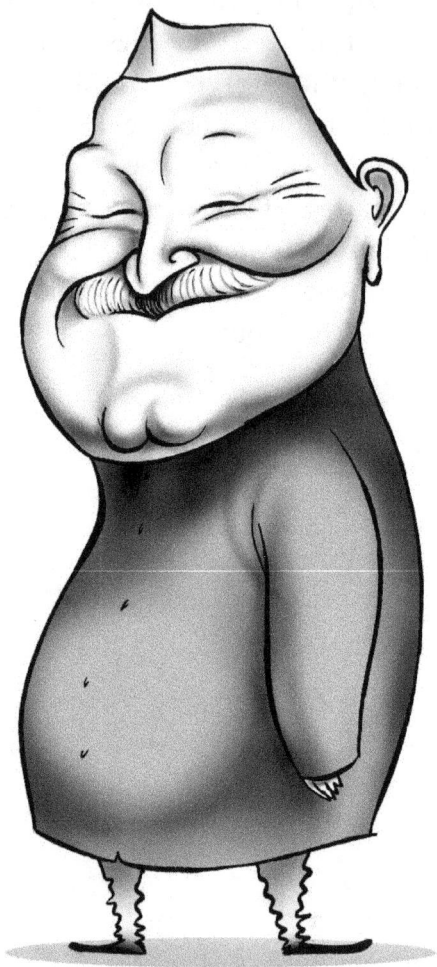

Shankar Dayal Sharma (1918–1999)

Professorial President
Shankar Dayal Sharma

Term of Office: 25 July 1992–25 July 1997

Rarely has a resident of Rashtrapati Bhavan been so richly distinguished by academic degrees, awards and acclaim as Shankar Dayal Sharma. During one period of his career, Sharma was chancellor of no less than twenty-two universities. His learning, distinction and academic experience made it natural for him to hold these posts.

The ninth president of the Indian republic, Shankar Dayal Sharma was born into a Brahmin family in Bhopal, Madhya Pradesh, on 19 August 1918. He received the best education at a number of distinguished institutions. He began his career from St John's College, Agra, later going on to study at Allahabad University, Lucknow University, Fitzwilliam College in Cambridge University, Lincoln's Inn and Harvard Law School.

One interesting feature of his student life was his prowess in sports. Apart from being an excellent student, Sharma was a keen sportsman. In his university career, he participated in athletics, rowing and swimming. While at Lucknow University, he was its swimming champion for three consecutive years and later became captain and then president of its Rowing and Swimming Club.

Acquiring a number of scholastic distinctions came easily to Sharma. He stood first in the university for all three of his MA degrees in English Literature, Hindi and Sanskrit. He repeated this feat for his LLM degree from Lucknow University. It seemed that few of his contemporaries could equal his passion or thirst for knowledge and scholarship. After completing these degrees, Sharma went on to study at institutions abroad. His PhD in law was obtained at Cambridge. Here, as in Lucknow University, he also taught law. While studying at Cambridge, Sharma was active in a number of student bodies. He was treasurer of the Tagore Society and the Cambridge Majlis. He became a practising lawyer in Lucknow in 1940 after being called to the Bar from Lincoln's Inn. Later, he became a Fellow at the Harvard Law School. His distinguished association with these institutions saw him being elected as an Honorary Bencher and Master of Lincoln's Inn and Honorary Fellow, Fitzwilliam College, Cambridge. The University of Cambridge honoured him with the degree of Doctor of Law (Honoris Causa). Another alma mater, Lucknow University, awarded him the Chakravarti Gold Medal for Social Service.

As a young lawyer in the days when patriots were being tried by the British for their involvement in the freedom struggle, Sharma was early on inspired by the Quit India Movement, in which he participated. This signalled the beginning of his social and political career. He served time in prison like hundreds of his contemporaries, fired by the desire for an independent nation, free from the shackles of foreign rule.

After independence, Shankar Dayal Sharma entered active electoral politics, being elected to the Bhopal Legislative Assembly. He was a member of this Assembly from 1952 to 1956. In 1956, he was elected to the Madhya Pradesh Legislative Assembly, and remained a member by subsequent re-elections till 1971. From 1971, he moved to the national arena by becoming an elected member of the fifth Lok Sabha from 1971 to 1977 and the seventh Lok Sabha from 1980 to1984.

During these years, Sharma was very active within the Congress party. He played an important role in building up the rank and file of the party through significant posts such as presidency of the Bhopal Congress Committee from 1950 to 1952 and the Madhya Pradesh Congress Committee from 1967 to 1968. He was general secretary of the Congress from 1968 to 1972, and had an uninterrupted stint as a member of the All India Congress Committee for more than thirty-two years from 1952 to 1984 and the Working Committee of the Congress for about twenty years. From 1972 to 1974, he was the president of the Indian National Congress.

His stellar role in the Congress party made it inevitable that he hold public office in various capacities. He was chief minister of the former state of Bhopal from 1952 to 1956. After this, he became a Cabinet minister in the government of Madhya Pradesh, holding such portfolios as Education, Law, Public Works, Industry and Commerce, National Resources and Separate

Revenue, from 1956 to 1967. After this, he served in the Centre as the Union minister for Communications from 1974 to 1977.

Alongside his career as a political leader, Sharma also had a very active and productive career in the academic field. From 1956 to 1959 he was pro-chancellor of Sagar University in Madhya Pradesh. He served as governor of three states: Andhra Pradesh, Punjab and Maharashtra. It was during these years that he was chancellor of twenty-two universities in those states and also rector of the University of Hyderabad.

From his appointments as governor of three states, Sharma went on to become the vice-president of India and chairman of the Rajya Sabha from 3 September 1987 till he assumed office as the president of India in 1992. When he was vice-president, he continued his academic involvement as the chancellor of Delhi University, Punjab University, Pondicherry University, Gandhigram Rural Institute (Deemed University), and Visitor of Makhanlal Chaturvedi Rashtriya Patrakarita Vishwavidyalaya Sansthan, Bhopal. He was also chairman of the Central Sanskrit Board.

Awarded many honorary degrees from universities as distant as the Kiev State University, Ukraine, as well as universities in Agra and

Roorkee, Mauritius and Romania, Sharma received rich recognition for his scholarship and for serving the cause of education and higher learning.

A man whose personality and character revealed his search for spiritual truths, Sharma was conferred the title of 'Rashtra Ratnam' or Jewel of the Nation by His Holiness the Shankaracharya of Sringeri. The title of 'Dharmaratnakara' was given to him by the high priest of Shravanbelagola.

The International Bar Association presented to Sharma the Living Legends of Law Award of Recognition for his outstanding contribution to the legal profession internationally and for commitment to the rule of law.

Keenly interested in several contemporary areas of development, Sharma followed events in these fields and wrote a number of books on international affairs, linguistics, law, philosophy, education, rural development and the comparative study of religions. *Congress Approach to International Affairs, Rule of Law and Role of Police, Secularism in the Indian Ethos, Horizons of Indian Education, The Democratic Process and Towards a New India* are some of the books he authored in English and Hindi.

This distinguished son of India passed away on 26 December 1999.

K.R. Narayanan (1920–2005)

Independent Thinker and Innovative President
K.R. Narayanan

Term of Office: 25 July 1997–25 July 2002

The last decade of the twentieth century saw India's politics sharply divided along the lines of the proponents of secularism versus those who opposed it as being 'pseudo-secularism'. This was a period that saw the rise of the Bharatiya Janata Party as a political force to be reckoned with since its birth in 1980. The 'rath yatra' that was undertaken by L.K. Advani in 1990 brought acceptance for primarily communal ideas and concepts even in the educated middle classes. At such a troubled period in modern Indian history, one president became recognised for his independent thinking and the accountability he brought to the presidential office by initiating a transparent method of decision-making. This president was K.R. or Kocheril Raman Narayanan, who assumed office as president of India on 25 July 1997.

Narayanan was born in the village of Uzhavoor in Kottayam district, Kerala. An interesting fact about his birth date is that he was actually born on 4 February 1921. However, an uncle who accompanied him to school on the first day couldn't remember his date of birth, so he randomly chose 27 October 1920. The date was mentioned in the official school records and remained, as Narayanan later decided to keep it.

Narayanan's father, Raman Vaidyan, was a Dalit practitioner of traditional medicine. Not only was the family placed on the lowest rung of the ladder of social discrimination practised in India as the hierarchical caste system, it was also very poor. Narayanan was the fourth of seven children. There were often occasions when there was not enough food for all of them to eat. This meant a life of grim struggle for the small boy. However, in a stirring example of how parents can work miracles for their children, his uneducated mother ensured that Narayanan was given a good education.

When he was four years old Narayanan was sent to the nearest English medium school – which was at a place called Kurichittanam, ten to fifteen kilometres from the village where he lived. His early life at school is a story of such Herculean effort that today's students would do well to remember how much some of our citizens have to struggle to get their primary education.

Narayanan first attended the Government Lower Primary School, Kurichittanam, where he studied from 1927 to 1931 and then Our Lady of Lourdes Upper Primary School, Uzhavoor, which he attended from 1931 to 1935. To get to school, he walked about fifteen kilometres every day, through paddy fields. Sometimes, when his father was unable to pay the modest fees, Narayanan would have to stand outside the classroom and listen to the school lessons, because only students who had paid their fees could enter the class. When there was no money to buy the textbooks that were needed, Narayanan's elder brother K.R. Neelakantan, who was often bedridden with asthma, would borrow books from other students and copy them out for Narayanan.

Apart from the difficulties of his own family, Narayanan had to cope with the lack of facilities at the schools where he studied. His science teacher would say to him, 'Imagine this is a test tube.' In spite of such challenging conditions, Narayanan was a good student who excelled at his studies and soon started financing his own education by winning scholarships that took him through high school and college. He matriculated from St Mary's High School in Kuravilangad in the academic year 1936–37, and completed his intermediate at CMS College, Kottayam, in 1940, aided by a merit scholarship.

His academic brilliance was further proved when he passed the BA (Literature) Honours examination from Maharaja's College in Thiruvananthapuram, winning the first rank in the University of Travancore (now the University of Kerala) in 1943. However, this victory was bittersweet. Having achieved such an important distinction, Narayanan faced the ugly nature of gross social discrimination. As the highest ranked student of his course, Narayanan should have got the job he wanted, which was that of a lecturer at Maharaja's College. But the authorities denied him the job as he belonged to a lower caste. Instead of the appointment, the then Chancellor offered him a clerical post in the university and a book worth Rs 100. Angry at such treatment, Narayanan demanded an audience with the maharaja of Travancore, who refused to see him. Narayanan protested against this patently unfair attitude of the college authorities by boycotting the convocation, and refusing to accept his degree.

In an ironic twist that was a tribute to his personal qualities of talent nurtured by unstinting hard work, this same university begged Narayanan to accept his degree fifty years later when he returned there to address a gathering. Fifty years after he had earned the degree, he agreed to receive it.

After his graduation, Narayanan worked for a while as a part-time teacher. His family was facing grave financial difficulties when he left for Delhi and began work as a journalist with the *Hindu* and the *Times of India* from 1944 to 1945. During this politically charged period, just a few years before Indian independence, Narayanan once interviewed Mahatma Gandhi in Bombay in April 1945.

An important period of Naryanan's life was just opening up. He was keen on going abroad to study, but unlike many of the leaders of the freedom struggle, an education abroad was unthinkable for a boy of his circumstances, whose family was so poor and disadvantaged. Moreover, there were hardly any scholarships available for deserving candidates in those days. At this point Narayanan wrote a letter to the eminent industrialist J.R.D. Tata asking him for a scholarship to help him study at the London School of Economics. J.R.D. came forward with the financial assistance he needed and Narayanan was able to study under the famous thinker Harold Laski and other important contemporary social scientists such as Karl Popper, Lionel Robbins and Friedrich Hayek.

Just as he had done in his earlier stint of academics, Narayanan obtained, with first class honours, the Honours degree of BSc (economics) with a specialisation in political science from the LSE. He had completed his three-year degree in just two years.

It was during these years that he spent in London that Narayanan was active in the India League under Indian nationalist and politician V.K. Krishna Menon along with fellow student K.N. Rai. He was the London correspondent of the *Social Welfare Weekly* published by K.M. Munshi, and shared lodgings with K.N. Rai and Veerasamy Ringadoo (who later became the first president of Mauritius). Another close friend from that time was Pierre Trudeau, who later became the prime minister of Canada.

Returning to India from London in 1948, he carried a letter of introduction from Harold Laski to the then prime minister Jawaharlal Nehru. Narayanan took the letter across and met Nehru for a personal interview that lasted a full twenty minutes. After their meeting Narayanan walked out to the corridor outside Nehru's office when he heard the sound of clapping. It was Nehru, calling him back after opening the letter that Narayanan had handed over to him just before leaving. 'You did not ask me what you wanted,' the prime minister said to Narayanan. 'What you wanted to do,' he added as gentle reminder. When he saw Narayanan hesitate, Nehru asked him to leave his resume and let him decide Narayanan's assignment. A little later, he offered Narayanan a job in the Indian Foreign Service and sent him to Burma.

Burma, now Myanmar, was in the midst of a civil war when Narayanan was posted there.

The talented young officer was almost prevented from making it to his first posting. His plane was rocking slightly while approaching Rangoon. When he finally landed, Narayanan learned that Karen rebels had shot at one of the plane's engines.

His posting in Rangoon, now Yangon, was to mark an important chapter in Narayanan's life. It was here that he met and married a young Myanmarese woman named Ma Trint Trint, who later took the name of Usha. The couple had two daughters, Chitra and Amrita.

Usha Narayanan accompanied her husband to many interesting and challenging assignments to different countries during his career in the Foreign Service. Narayanan served in Indian embassies in Rangoon, Tokyo, London, Canberra and Hanoi, and held different positions in the ministry of External Affairs. He was India's ambassador to Thailand from 1967 to 1969, Turkey from 1973 to 1975, the People's Republic of China from 1976 to 1978 and secretary in the ministry of External Affairs.

Between these assignments he was persuaded to teach economic administration at the Delhi School of Economics from 1954 to 1955 and was also the joint director of the Orientation Centre for Foreign Technicians.

An important academic appointment awaited Narayanan when he retired from the Foreign Service in 1978. He was appointed vice-chancellor of the prestigious Jawaharlal Nehru University. However, his diplomatic services would soon be recalled for the country. In 1980, the then prime minister Indira Gandhi recalled him to active service and appointed him ambassador to the United States of America, an important post that he held for four years.

From 1984 Narayanan plunged into popular politics and was elected to the Lok Sabha from the Ottapalam constituency in Kerala. He was re-elected from this same constituency in the 1989 and 1991 general elections. Narayanan served as the minister of State for Planning, External Affairs, and Science and Technology in Rajiv Gandhi's government.

Narayanan's path to Rashtrapati Bhavan began in 1992 when he was elected the vice-president of India. He occupied this post from 21 August 1992 to July 1997 when he was elected the tenth president of the country, winning with ninety-five per cent of the votes, and comfortably defeating his presidential election opponent, the former election commissioner T.N. Seshan.

As the president of the Republic of India, Narayanan's tenure was marked by several important decisions and actions that set him apart from being a mere 'rubber-stamp' president – one who does the bidding of the prime minister and council of ministers. He proved that the president has the Constitutional duty to apply his or her mind to each decision and weigh its pros and cons for the benefit of the country.

In his five years in office, Narayanan joined other citizens at a polling booth to cast his vote during a general election – showing that a president shares the duty of ordinary citizens as well, and can have his own personal political preference, even if he is above party politics. He used his discretionary powers to innovate and improvise, and his diplomatic skills to break new ground with China at a difficult time in the relations between the two countries. He twice returned for reconsideration questionable Union Cabinet decisions. In October 1997, the Inder Kumar Gujral government was forced to reconsider its decision to dismiss Uttar Pradesh chief minister Kalyan Singh, and in September 1998, after the president sent back a notification, the Vajpayee government went back on its decision to dismiss the Rabri Devi government in Bihar.

This president worked within the parameters of the Indian Constitution, but he never allowed concerns of propriety, or what had been done by other presidents in the past, to divert him from what he saw as his social mission, or the dictates of his own conscience. Nehru had once called Narayanan 'the best diplomat of the country'. However, he never hesitated to speak straight from the heart: when the Babri Masjid was demolished on 6 December 1992, he described the event as the 'greatest tragedy India has faced since the assassination of Mahatma Gandhi'. Again, when Australian missionary and social worker Graham Staines and his two minor sons were burned alive in January 1999, Narayanan condemned it as a barbarous crime belonging to the world's inventory of black deeds. When his presidential term was nearing completion, communal riots broke out in Gujarat in February 2002. This was a source of deep pain and anguish for the president and he described it as a grave crisis of the society and the nation, calling upon every Indian to strive to restore peace and thus preserve and strengthen the foundations of the State and the tradition of tolerance. He also tried to get the Indian Army to intervene and protect the minority Muslim population – a move that was not accepted by the country's ruling Bharatiya Janata Party.

Narayanan was impatient to achieve social and economic justice for the poor, and made a strong case for giving a sense of economic liberation to the masses through land reform. Not forgetful of his humble origins that had exposed him to discrimination, Narayanan said, 'My elevation to high office should not be seen as a personal achievement but as an instance in history where a person becomes a symbol of the hope and aspirations of thousands of people in the country.' In many of his speeches, Narayanan consistently sought to remind the nation of its duties and obligations towards Dalits and Adivasis, the minorities, the poor and downtrodden.

In another remarkable departure from convention, throughout his presidency Narayanan adopted a policy of not visiting places of worship or being seen paying homage to any godman/godwoman. He is the only president to have followed this practice, a measure of his independent thinking and his reluctance to encourage further superstition and blind belief among the people.

Narayanan was awarded the Jawaharlal Nehru Fellowship in 1970–72 for a study of Pandit Nehru's Non-alignment, and received the World Statesman Award of the Appeal of Conscience Foundation, New York in 1998. This distinguished president was a patron of many cultural, social and literary organisations, and was joined in his social engagements by his wife, herself an active social worker closely involved in welfare activities for women and children. A writer on social and political issues, Narayanan authored books such as *India and America: Essays in Understanding, Non-alignment in Contemporary International Relations* and *Nehru and His Vision.*

K.R. Narayanan died on 9 November 2005, at the age of eighty-five, at the Army Research and Referral Hospital, New Delhi, after a brief illness. The outpouring of grief and affection from all over the country and abroad overwhelmed his family, leading his daughter Chitra, now in the Indian Foreign Service, to respond with the words that her father K.R. Narayanan would be remembered for his great love for the nation and for his immense moral strength and courage.

If anything illustrates the long journey travelled by this illustrious son of India, it is the contrast between Uzhavoor, the place where Narayanan was born in Kerala, and Rashtrapati Bhavan. Uzhavoor is a tiny dot on the map. Narayanan's home, House No. 456 in Ward 5, was a small hut on a hill, with a thatched roof, two small rooms and a tiny kitchen. In his childhood, this humble home had no electricity or telephone connection, no water supply and no toilet.

When Narayanan became the deserving occupant of Rashtrapati Bhavan, he lived in a 340-room palace, one of the largest official residences in the world. This residence boasts of the famous Mughal Gardens, nine tennis courts, a fourteen-hole golf course, polo ground and cricket field, with extensive grounds that have been developed into a man-made forest.

About his own life and the journey from Uzhavoor to the presidency, K.R. Narayanan said, 'I see and understand both the symbolic as well as the substantive elements of my life. Sometimes I visualise it as a journey of an individual from a remote village on the sidelines of society to the hub of social standing. But at the same time I also realise that my life encapsulates the ability of the democratic system to accommodate and empower marginalised sections of society.'

A.P.J. Abdul Kalam (b. 1931)

The People's President
A.P.J. Abdul Kalam

Term of Office: 25 July 2002–25 July 2007

When the eleventh president of the Republic of India was sworn in, many wondered at how this non-political person, who had never fought an election in his life, would fare in a constitutional post. But Dr A.P.J. Abdul Kalam was not only one of the most popular presidents the country has seen, he also brought to this august post an accessibility that has since become a benchmark.

Dr Avul Pakir Jainulabdeen Abdul Kalam was born on 15 October 1931 at Rameswaram in Tamil Nadu. His father, Jainulabdeen, owned several boats in this seaside town. His mother's name was Ashiamma, and he had many siblings.

The family lived on Mosque Street, like many other Muslims in the town, but Kalam's childhood was unique for several reasons. One was that his father, a very devout person, also happened to be a close friend of Pakshi Lakshmana Sastry, the head priest of the famous Rameswaram Siva temple. Sastry's son sat on the same bench as Kalam at school. While both families were pious followers of their respective religions, they also had tremendous respect for the faith of the other. Abdul Kalam's father instilled in his son a respect for true human values by explaining religious concepts to him in simple terms. Abdul Kalam thus grew up with a deep respect for the values that are common to all faiths.

Another unique aspect of Abdul Kalam's childhood was the caring and guidance he received from an elder friend, Ahmed Jalaluddin. The attachment between the two began when Abdul Kalam was a mere six years old and Jalaluddin was twenty-one, and continued aided by Jalaluddin's marriage to Zohara, Kalam's sister. The two friends roamed the island of Rameswaram, discussing every conceivable subject, and often visited the large Siva temple to sit or walk within its welcoming precincts.

Kalam earned his first wages by helping his relative Samsuddin deliver newspapers during the Second World War. He was first exposed to a large-scale tragedy when a cyclone struck Rameswaram and destroyed his father's boat business. During this calamity, the famous Pamban bridge collapsed, plunging a trainload of passengers into the ocean. Truly philosophical, Jainulabdeen considered his personal tragedy considerably less important than the larger one.

Even from these earliest times, Abdul Kalam wanted to fly like a bird, something he has described in touching detail in his autobiography *Wings of Fire*. On his quest for such a future, he attended Schwartz High School at Ramanathapuram and St Joseph's College at Trichy. In both places, he had excellent teachers and showed an aptitude for mathematics. He specialised in Aeronautical Engineering from the Madras Institute of Technology.

However, his ambition to be a pilot was dashed when he did not clear an interview with the Indian Air Force after graduating from MIT. He was set to become something completely different – a rocket scientist. This began with his appointment as senior scientific assistant in the Directorate of

Technical Development and Production (Air) of the ministry of Defence. He began work in 1958 at a monthly salary of Rs 250.

Kalam's work of developing rocket launchers brought him in contact with Vikram Sarabhai, then India's foremost space scientist. Dr Kalam grew to admire tremendously the character and leadership qualities of Dr Sarabhai. The latter's untimely death saddened him and was a personal setback.

Later, Kalam became the project director of India's first indigenous Satellite Launch Vehicle (SLV-III) which successfully launched the Rohini satellite into orbit in July 1980. He worked for two decades at ISRO or the Indian Space Research Organisation, and was responsible for the evolution of ISRO's launch vehicle programme, the PSLV. He was then picked for developing Indigenous Guided Missiles at DRDO or the Defence Research and Development Organisation as the chief executive of the Integrated Guided Missile Development Programme (IGMDP).

Kalam's leadership was critical in the development and operations of the Agni and Prithvi missiles. He was the scientific advisor to the Defence minister and secretary, Department of Defence Research & Development, from July 1992 to December 1999. It was during this period that the Pokhran-II nuclear tests were conducted. India's self-reliance in defence systems also gained momentum through Kalam's efforts by the development of mission projects such as Light Combat Aircraft.

Dr Kalam developed a blueprint for India's development called Technology Vision 2020 as chairman of the Technology Information, Forecasting and Assessment Council (TIFAC) with the help of 500 experts. He was the principal scientific advisor to the Government of India, in the rank of Cabinet minister, from November 1999 to November 2001, which made him responsible for evolving policies and strategies for many development applications. Another appointment was the chairman, Ex-officio, of the Scientific Advisory Committee to the Cabinet (SAC-C), which led to him piloting the India Millennium Mission 2020.

Kalam has had an academic career as the professor, Technology and Societal Transformation at Anna University, Chennai, from November 2001 and has returned to this campus after completing his term as president. This has made it possible for him to be actively involved in teaching and research and the igniting of young minds for national development. He has also reached out to the larger public with his books – the best-selling *Wings of Fire* and *India 2020 – A Vision for the New Millennium*, *My Journey* and *Ignited Minds – Unleashing the Power within India*. These books have been translated into several Indian languages.

One of the most distinguished names among Indian scientists, Kalam has the unique honour of receiving honorary doctorates from thirty universities and institutions. He was awarded the Padma Bhushan in 1981, the Padma Vibhushan in 1990 and India's highest civilian award, the Bharat Ratna, in 1997.

Kalam's term as the eleventh president of India opened Rashtrapati Bhavan to common Indian citizens in a way that had not been seen in recent years. Considering the importance of children for the future of the country, Kalam set out to meet over one lakh of them during his term. By the time he stepped down he had met over five lakh children! He engaged them in conversation and encouraged them to dream in a way few politicians do. It is no wonder that he developed a huge fan following among children, for whom he provided a direct contrast from their often cynical parents.

Keen on using the amenities of Rashtrapati Bhavan to benefit the people, Dr Kalam had a medicinal herb garden planted here to assist research in the healing properties of plants. He lived a very simple life himself, eating a simple vegetarian diet and enjoying a number of hobbies like playing classical Carnatic music on the veena in his leisure time. Kalam is a deeply spiritual person who writes poetry in his mother tongue, Tamil.

Kalam earned the abiding respect of the people of India by his inspiring patriotism and his actions as the president of millennial India. The epithet by which he came to be known – the 'People's President' – is a true, fitting sign of how citizens came to regard him.

Pratibha Devisingh Patil (b. 1934)

First Woman President
Pratibha Devisingh Patil

Term of Office: 25 July 2007 till date

Pratibha Devisingh Patil was sworn in as the twelfth president of India on 25 July 2007. Before this she had been the governor of Rajasthan from 8 November 2004 till 21 June 2007. Patil, who had been a member of the Indian National Congress for many years, was nominated by the ruling United Progressive Alliance supported by the Communist parties. She won the presidential election held on 19 July 2007, defeating her nearest rival Bhairon Singh Shekhawat by over 300,000 votes.

In this victory, Patil was underlining another unique aspect of her life. Becoming a legislator at the young age of twenty-seven in the Maharashtra

Assembly, she has been a member of both the Lok Sabha and the Rajya Sabha and has never been defeated in any election in which she has stood.

Patil was born on 19 December 1934 in Nadgaon village of Jalgaon district, Maharashtra. Her early years were spent in Jalgaon town, where she completed her education — first at R.R. Vidyalaya, and later, up to her Master's degree in political science and economics from Mooljee Jetha College. It was here, in 1962, that she was voted 'College Queen'. The same year Patil won an Assembly election from Jalgaon and became an MLA. After her graduation, Patil enrolled for her Bachelor of Law (LLB) degree from Government Law College, Mumbai. Although she was now a legislator, she pursued her studies and completed her degree. She also found the time to take an active part in sports, excelling in table tennis and winning several shields at various inter-collegiate tournaments.

After getting her LLB degree, Patil began practising law at the Jalgaon district court. She married educator Devisingh Ramsingh Shekhawat, a Rajput from Rajasthan, on 7 July 1965. The couple was well-matched in their desire for active social service, especially in the field of education and the uplifting of poor women. They have a daughter, Jyoti Rathore, and a son, Rajendra Singh.

Edlabad, or Muktai Nagar in Jalgaon district, remained Patil's constituency from 1967 right up till 1985. She was elected four times from here to the Maharashtra Assembly. During this long period, she held various important positions both in the government and the Legislative Assembly of Maharashtra. Pratibha Patil's political career began under the mentorship of senior Congress leader and former chief minister Yashwantrao Chavan. She began by becoming a deputy minister for Education in 1967 in the Vasantrao Naik ministry. In her next terms between 1972 and 1978 she was a full Cabinet minister for the state. Various important portfolios like Tourism, Social Welfare and Housing were handled by her in the successive governments of Vasantdada Patil, Babasaheb Bhosle, S.B. Chavan and Sharad Pawar.

The Congress party, which has seen several splinter groups break away from it in the post-Independence era, split up in 1977 in Maharashtra after Indira Gandhi's defeat in the general elections following the Emergency of 1975 to 1977. During this split, many senior leaders like Y.B. Chavan and his protégé Sharad Pawar joined the Congress (U) party floated by Devraj Urs. However, at this time, and on all subsequent occasions, Patil remained loyal to Indira Gandhi, although she was taking a political risk by antagonising other Maharashtra stalwarts.

Patil's belief in Indira Gandhi, and her unshakable loyalty, was immense. One lesser known fact was her quiet support to Indira Gandhi when her son Sanjay Gandhi died in an air crash. In the hours following the tragedy, Patil quietly managed Indira Gandhi's kitchen and household. When Indira Gandhi was arrested in 1977 by a government thirsting to avenge the repression and humiliation of the Emergency, Patil took part in a protest, for which she had to spend ten days in prison.

From 1978, when the Congress (U) came to power in Maharashtra, she became the Leader of the Opposition in the state Assembly, and later chief of the Maharashtra Pradesh Congress Committee.

Patil's political career had grown alongside the work she and her husband were doing for women and disadvantaged groups. The couple set up an educational institution called Vidya Bharati Shikshan Prasarak Mandal, which runs a chain of schools and colleges in Jalgaon and Mumbai. Patil also set up the Shram Sadhana Trust that runs hostels for working women in New Delhi, Mumbai and Pune and an engineering college in Jalgaon. Other institutions she has been a part of are the cooperative sugar factory known as Sant Muktabai Sahakari Sakhar Karkhana, of which she has been the chairperson, and a cooperative bank called the Pratibha Mahila Sahakari Bank, named after her. Patil set up an industrial training school for the visually challenged in Jalgaon and a school for the poor children of vimukta jatis or nomadic tribes.

It was her work in the social arena that got Patil elected to the Rajya Sabha in 1985 as a Congress candidate. In the Rajya Sabha, Patil served as the deputy chairperson from 1986 to 1988 and as the chairperson for a short period in 1987 from July to September when R. Venkataraman was elected as the president of India. In 1991 she contested the general elections from the Amaravati constituency for the Lok Sabha and was elected MP to the tenth Lok Sabha.

Her social work and association with institutions furthering the cause of women and the less privileged has meant that Patil represented India abroad on various occasions. Notably, she was present at the International Council on Social Welfare conferences at Nairobi and at Puerto Rico. In 1985 she accompanied the AICC (I) delegation to Bulgaria in 1985 and in 1988 she went to London as part of the Commonwealth Presiding Officers Conference. She led the Indian delegation to the conference on the 'Status of Women' in Austria and was a delegate at the World Women's Conference, Beijing, in September 1995.

From 2004 to 2007 Patil was governor of Rajasthan, leaving her post only because she was nominated for the post of president by the ruling UPA. On 14 June 2007, this ruling alliance of political parties nominated her as their candidate for the presidential election to be held on 19 July 2007. She emerged as a compromise candidate after the Communist parties who supported the UPA government did not agree to the nomination of then Home minister Shivraj Patil. Patil's name was proposed by Indian National Congress president Sonia Gandhi. Critics of this choice alleged that Sonia Gandhi had put forward the name only because Patil's loyalty to the Nehru-Gandhi family was well-known, and had been proved and tested in many circumstances.

Patil, who asserted at the beginning of her presidency that she would not be a 'rubber-stamp' president, had the tough job of following the vibrant and widely popular term of president A.P.J. Abdul Kalam. She also had the task of proving that she was not carrying the tag of 'woman president' without adding any value to the president's post on account of her gender. After her election, the bitter political atmosphere that had surrounded Sonia Gandhi's choice of presidential candidate continued. Patil became embroiled in a controversy for her quotes about purdah and her claim of having silent communion with the spirit of a dead 'Baba'. Her family members' misdemeanours and various cases filed against them were also widely discussed. She survived the initial months of her presidency in the background of all these controversies.

Her subsequent actions have showed president Patil to be keenly responsive to present-day development and her countrymen's needs. 'Terrorism and communal hatred are enemies of development, stability and a peaceful society,' she said on 23 September 2008 in Lucknow after receiving the D.Litt degree conferred on her by Lucknow University. Patil praised the security and police personnel engaged in fighting terrorism, and said that 'It is the duty of every citizen of the country to co-operate in combating terrorism'.

'We have to divest hatred from the minds of some of our misguided youth and bring them to the path of peace, amity and communal harmony,' she further added. Later, regretting the decline in the country's research facilities, Patil said that research facilities in our universities need to be reinforced. She described India as committed to building and improving its infrastructure facilities and ensuring health, education and connectivity across the country.

As twenty-first century India moves forward to a greater global presence, Patil has the opportunity to bring meaning and importance to the role of the Indian president.

www.ingramcontent.com/pod-product-compliance
Lightning Source LLC
LaVergne TN
LVHW052030080426
835513LV00018B/2260